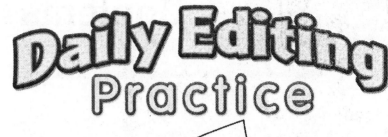

Editor
Eric Migliaccio

Managing Editor
Ina Massler Levin, M.A.

Editor-in-Chief
Sharon Coan, M.S. Ed.

Cover Artist
Barb Lorseyedi

Art Coordinator
Kevin Barnes

Art Director
CJae Froshay

Imaging
Craig Gunnell

Product Manager
Phil Garcia

Author

Janelle Condra, M.A. Ed.

Publisher
Mary D. Smith, M.S. Ed.

Teacher Created Resources, Inc.
6421 Industry Way
Westminster, CA 92683
www.teachercreated.com
ISBN: 978-0-7439-3222-6
©2004 Teacher Created Resources, Inc.
Reprinted, 2008
Made in U.S.A.

Table of Contents

Table of Contents

Introduction

About This Book

Purpose

The purpose of the *Daily Editing Practice* program is to introduce, review, and practice basic language concepts needed to develop proficient writing skills. This consistent and frequent guided practice promotes skill mastery that will carry over to other writing assignments.

This resource is designed as a ready-to-use daily language program. It can be used in the form of a consumable workbook or as individual reproducible worksheets. It is meant to be used in a guided group lesson and consists mainly of sentences written incorrectly followed by blank lines provided for the students to rewrite the corrected sentence.

Included at the beginning of units 1–6 is a list of language rules explaining each new skill that will be presented. There are nine units, with 20 sentences per unit. Each unit provides daily practice for four weeks. Sentences become longer and skills more complex throughout the book. Assessment pages are included after each unit to check progress. In addition, all skills introduced in a unit are periodically reviewed throughout the following units to reinforce and master skills taught. A cumulative assessment of all skills presented in the book is also included. An overview of skills taught and reinforced is provided on the Scope & Sequence Skills Chart (page 6).

A page with blank writing lines is included for teachers to write their own sentences. This may be done for additional practice with specific skills or to individualize sentences. The answer keys provided can be torn out if the book is being used as a consumable workbook.

Skill Rules

At the beginning of units 1–6, any new skill presented is included on a "Rules to Know" page. Using these rules as guides, short lessons can be provided as needed by the teacher when introducing a new skill. These rules are not meant to be taught all at once, but individually as they come up in the unit sentences. If the book is not being used as a consumable workbook, these rule pages can be copied and given to students as skills are introduced. Students can keep these pages together in a folder or booklet as their own individual language skills rule book, to be reviewed or referred to as needed. In units 7–9, no new skills are presented. These units provide review and practice of previous skills taught.

Standards Alignment

State standards in the language arts/writing area for primary grades emphasize conventions of print and editing written work using correct letter formation, spacing, grammar, punctuation, capitalization, and spelling. This is exactly what the *Daily Editing Practice* program provides. Teachers will be meeting standards requirements, while providing consistent and frequent practice leading to mastery and retention of needed skills for developing writers.

Introduction
(cont.)

Practice Sentences

Most practice pages have two sentences. If the book is not being used as a consumable workbook, sheets can be copied and cut in half. The teacher passes out the sentence sheet for the day to each student and writes the same sentence on the board. The sentence is then read together out loud and the class, as a group, corrects the sentence. The teacher asks for correction ideas from the students and makes changes to the sentence written on the board as students come up with correct responses. For every correction, the reason for the correction is given as well as how to make the needed change. Conventions of print in writing such as correct letter formation and proper spacing should also be emphasized. Any dates used can be part of the corrections to reflect the current year.

As the teacher corrects each error on the board, the students correct the same errors on their papers. Finally, the students independently rewrite the sentence on the blank lines below. The following is an example of how students make corrections to a sentence during a guided group lesson.

$$D \qquad\qquad to \quad W \qquad\qquad S$$

do you go two westside school?

Assessment

The skill assessment pages are meant to be used at the end of each unit and consist of three of the practice sentences from that unit. On these pages, the teacher reads each sentence to the class and the students independently make corrections to the sentences without recopying them. This gives the teacher a way to assess students progress and determine the need for any additional reinforcement to the class or individual student in specific skill areas. The points possible represent the total number of words, groups of numbers, and punctuation marks in the three sentences and are indicated on the assessment page. Each word, group of numbers, and punctuation mark is awarded one point and is counted as either totally correct or incorrect. This means counting all words, numbers, and punctuation whether incorrectly written or not. For example, if a student capitalizes a word that does not need to be capitalized, it would be counted as wrong, even though it is written correctly in the sentence above. The total number of possible points for each unit assessment is calculated and written at the bottom of each assessment page.

The cumulative assessment includes a sample of all skills presented in the book. Since this assessment is much longer, having students complete it in more than one session is recommended.

Scope & Sequence Skills Chart

• = Skill Introduced
+ = Skill Reinforced

	Units								
	1	2	3	4	5	6	7	8	9
Capitalization									
Beginning of a sentence	•	+	+	+	+	+	+	+	+
The word I	•	+	+	+	+	+	+	+	+
Proper nouns	•	+	+	+	+	+	+	+	+
Days of the week	•	+	+	+	+	+	+	+	+
Months of the year	•	+	+	+	+	+	+	+	+
Name title	•	+	+	+	+	+	+	+	+
Holidays	•	+	+	+	+	+	+	+	+
Book title		•	+	+	+	+	+	+	+
Relationship nouns			•	+	+	+	+	+	+
First word in a quote			•	+	+	+	+	+	+
Letter greeting/closing				•	+	+	+	+	+
Address				•	+	+	+	+	+
Punctuation									
Sentence ending period	•	+	+	+	+	+	+	+	+
Sentence ending question mark	•	+	+	+	+	+	+	+	+
Period in an abbreviation	•	+	+	+	+	+	+	+	+
Comma in a date	•	+	+	+	+	+	+	+	+
Apostrophe in a singular possessive	•	+	+	+	+	+	+	+	+
Commas in a series	•	+	+	+	+	+	+	+	+
Comma between city and state	•	+	+	+	+	+	+	+	+
Sentence ending exclamation mark	•	+	+	+	+	+	+	+	+
Underline in a title		•	+	+	+	+	+	+	+
Apostrophe in a contraction		•	+	+	+	+	+	+	+
Colon/time		•	+	+	+	+	+	+	+
Quotation marks			•	+	+	+	+	+	+
Comma in letter greeting/closing			•	+	+	+	+	+	+
Apostrophe in a plural possessive			•	+	+	+	+	+	+
Comma in a quotation				•	+	+	+	+	+
Comma in a compound sentence					•	+	+	+	+
Comma after yes/no						•	+	+	+
Grammar & Usage									
Homophones	•	+	+	+	+	+	+	+	+
Add s or es to make nouns plurals	•	+	+	+	+	+	+	+	+
Word order	•	+	+	+	+	+	+	+	+
Pronoun usage	•	+	+	+	+	+	+	+	+
Verb tenses		•	+	+	+	+	+	+	+
Misspelled/misused verbs		•	+	+	+	+	+	+	+
Subject/verb agreement		•	+	+	+	+	+	+	+
Irregular past tense verbs			•	+	+	+	+	+	+
Irregular plural nouns			•	+	+	+	+	+	+
Double subjects				•	+	+	+	+	+
Double negatives				•	+	+	+	+	+
Using a or an					•	+	+	+	+
Run-on Sentence					•	+	+	+	+
Comparative/superlative endings						•	+	+	+

Unit 1
Rules to Know

1. A sentence is a group of words that tells a complete thought. Capitalize the first word in a sentence.

   ➢ **<u>T</u>he dog is black.**

2. Capitalize the word I.

   ➢ **Tom and <u>I</u> are friends.**

3. *Nouns* are words that name people, places, things, and animals. Proper nouns name specific people, places, things, and animals and begin with a capital letter. Capitalize the names of people, pets, and specific places.

   ➢ **I will play with <u>D</u>an and <u>P</u>uff.**

   ➢ **Is <u>P</u>ark <u>S</u>chool on <u>M</u>aple <u>S</u>treet?**

   ➢ **We went to <u>F</u>lorida on vacation.**

4. A statement is a sentence that tells something. Put a period at the end of a telling sentence. A question is a sentence that asks something. Put a question mark at the end of an asking sentence. An exclamation is a sentence that expresses strong feeling. It ends with an exclamation mark.

   ➢ **My house is white<u>.</u>**

   ➢ **Do you have a pet<u>?</u>**

   ➢ **We won the game<u>!</u>**

5. Capitalize the days of the week, months of the year, and holidays.

   ➢ **My birthday is on a <u>S</u>aturday in <u>M</u>ay.**

   ➢ **We have a big meal on <u>T</u>hanksgiving.**

6. An abbreviation is a short form of a word. Capitalize name titles and put a period after ones that have been shortened into an abbreviation.

   Mister — Mr.   *Misses — Mrs.*   *Doctor — Dr.*

   ➢ **His friend is <u>Mr.</u> Brown.**

   ➢ **My teacher is <u>Mrs.</u> Lee.**

   ➢ **<u>Dr.</u> Rob is at the hospital.**

   ➢ **<u>Miss</u> Smith lives here.**

7. A possessive noun shows ownership. Use an apostrophe and an *s* ('s) after a noun to show something belongs to one person or thing.

   ➢ **That is Beth<u>'s</u> room.**

   ➢ **My dog<u>'s</u> name is Pal.**

8. A *homophone* is a word that sounds the same as another word but has a different spelling or meaning. Use the homophones *to*, *two*, and *too* correctly.

   <u>to</u> — in the direction of   <u>two</u> — names a number   <u>too</u> — also or more than enough

   ➤ **I went <u>to</u> school.**   ➤ **That box is <u>too</u> heavy to lift.**
   ➤ **Did you read <u>two</u> books?**   ➤ **She wants some candy, <u>too</u>.**

9. A comma signals a pause. Use a comma in a date to separate the day and year. Use a comma to separate a city and state.

   ➤ **She was born on September 10, 2003.**
   ➤ **Do you live in Dallas, Texas?**

10. A *series* is a list of three or more items. Use a comma to separate three or more words, or groups of words in a series.

    ➤ **Is your favorite food pizza, hamburger, or macaroni?**
    ➤ **At the zoo he saw a tiger, an elephant, and a bear.**

11. A *pronoun* is a word that is used in place of a noun. Use the pronouns *they* and *them* correctly.

    use *they* — when a group is doing something
    use *them* — when something is happening to a group

    ➤ **<u>They</u> are going home.**
    ➤ **Will you help <u>them</u>?**

12. A *subject* tells who or what the sentence is about. In a sentence with more than one subject where the pronoun *I* or *me* is used, *I* or *me* is written last.

    use *I* when you are doing something

    use *me* when something happens to you

    ➤ **<u>Tim and I</u> went to the movie.**
    ➤ **She gave it to <u>Bob and me</u>.**

13. A *singular noun* names one person, place, thing, or animal. A *plural noun* names more than one person, place, thing, or animal.

    Add *s* to most nouns to make them plural.

    Add *es* to words that end in *s, ch, sh, x,* and *z.*

    ➤ **Where are the dog<u>s</u>?**
    ➤ **The dish<u>es</u> need to be washed.**

this year i am in the second grade

This year I am in the second grade.

where did you go in july

Where did you go in July?

Name: _____ Date: _9/3/08_

my teacher is mrs

carson

My teacher is Mrs.
Carson.

Name: _____ Date: _____

do you go two westside

school

Do you go two Westside
School?

tom jill and bob are

coming on friday

Tom, Jill, and Bob are

coming on Friday.

my friend jays pet is

a cat named fluff

My friend Jays pet is

a Cat named Fluff.

flag day was on
june 14 2004

Flag day was on
June 14, 2004.

me and my mom live
in miami florida

Me and my mom live
in Miami, Florida.

bill potters house is
on fire

Bill Potters house is
on fire!   ?

---

did them get too cat
last saturday

Did they get two cats
last Saturday.?

does fall begin in

september or october

Does fall begin in

September Or

October?

have you ever been

two reno nevada

Have you ever been

to reno nevada?

Reno, Nevada

on monday i got to
box in the mail

On Monday I got two
boxis in the mail.

will jim help me
and sam

Will Jim help me and
Sam?

was your birthday in

june july or august

W your birthday in

June, July, or August?

miss smith went too

canada last summer

Miss Smith went too

Canada last

summer.

was amber born on

august 1 2004

Was Amber born on

August 1, 2004?

---

on saturday we went

too my brothers game

On Saturday we went

too my brothers

game.

did school start in

august or september

Did school start in

August or September?

my to favorite fruits

are apples and peachs

My to favorit

fruits are apples

and peachs.

Unit 1 — Assessment

Name: _Christiana_   Date: _9/16/08_

1. do you go two to
Westside school?

2. tom, jill, and Bob are
coming on friday.

3. Bill potters house is
on fire.

Good job!

Score all words, group of numbers, or punctuation marks in these sentences as one point each, whether or not a correction is needed.

Score: _____ /26 _____ %

Unit 1 — Assessment

Answer Key

1. $\overset{D}{\underset{\rule{1.5em}{0.4pt}}{do}}$ you go $\overset{to}{\underset{\rule{1.5em}{0.4pt}}{two}}$ $\overset{W}{\underset{\rule{1.5em}{0.4pt}}{westside}}$ $\overset{S}{\underset{\rule{1.5em}{0.4pt}}{school?}}$

2. $\overset{T}{\underset{\rule{1.5em}{0.4pt}}{tom,}}$ $\overset{J}{\underset{\rule{1.5em}{0.4pt}}{jill,}}$ and $\overset{B}{\underset{\rule{1.5em}{0.4pt}}{bob}}$ are coming on $\overset{F}{\underset{\rule{1.5em}{0.4pt}}{friday.}}$

3. $\overset{B}{\underset{\rule{1.5em}{0.4pt}}{bill}}$ $\overset{P}{\underset{\rule{1.5em}{0.4pt}}{potter's}}$ house is on fire!

Unit 1
Answer Key

1. This year I am in the second grade.

2. Where did you go in July?

3. My teacher is Mrs. Carson.

4. Do you go to Westside School?***

5. Tom, Jill, and Bob are coming on Friday.***

6. My friend Jay's pet is a cat named Fluff.

7. Flag Day was on June 14, 2004.

8. My mom and I live in Miami, Florida.

9. Bill Potter's house is on fire!***

10. Did they get two cats last Saturday?

11. Does fall begin in September or October?

12. Have you ever been to Reno, Nevada?

13. On Monday I got two boxes in the mail.

14. Will Jim help Sam and me?

15. Was your birthday in June, July, or August?

16. Miss Smith went to Canada last summer.

17. Was Amber born on August 1, 2004?

18. On Saturday we went to my brother's game.

19. Did school start in August or September?

20. My two favorite fruits are apples and peaches.

*** **Unit 1 Assessment answers**

Unit 2
Rules to Know

1. A *homophone* is a word that sounds the same as another word but has a different spelling or meaning. Learn to use homophones correctly. Here are some examples:

red / read	their / there / they're	weak / week
be / bee	knight / night	buy / by
knew / new	here / hear	would / wood
sea / see	to / two / too	for / four
one / won	know / no	rode / road

2. A *colon* is used between the hour and minutes when writing the time of day.

   ➤ **We went to school at 8:00.**
   ➤ **In two hours it will be 3:00.**

3. A *contraction* is a word made by joining two words. When joining the words, a letter or letters are left out. An apostrophe is put in the word at the spot where the letter or letters are missing.

   ➤ **We are going home.** → **We're going home.**
   ➤ **She did not see him.** → **She didn't see him.**
   ➤ **He will be there soon.** → **He'll be there soon.**

4. A *pronoun* is a word that is used in place of a noun. Use the pronouns *we/us*, *she/he*, and *her/him* correctly.

   use *we* — when you and others are doing something
   use *she/he* — when a person is doing something
   use *us* — when something happens to you and others
   use *her/him* — when something happens to a person

   ➤ **We went to school.**　　➤ **They gave the trophy to us.**
   ➤ **He is riding the bike.**　　➤ **She will cook dinner.**
   ➤ **Sam gave him a ride.**　　➤ **Bill took her to the movie.**

5. When writing the title of a book, underline the entire title and capitalize the first word, the last word, and each important word.

> **Have you read the book <u>Hansel and Gretel</u>?**

> **<u>Little Red Riding Hood</u> is my favorite book.**

6. *A present tense* verb shows action that happens now. *A past tense* verb tells about an action that already happened. Add *–ed* to most verbs to form past tense. If the verb has a single vowel and ends with a consonant, double the last consonant before adding *–ed*. If it ends with *e*, drop the final e and add *–ed*.

> **(paint) Yesterday he <u>painted</u> the house.**

> **(hop) The rabbit <u>hopped</u> away.**

> **(like) They <u>liked</u> their new school.**

7. The verbs *am, are, is, was,* and *were* are not action words. Instead, they tell what someone or something is like.

Use *am* with the word *I*.

Use *is* and *are* when talking about what is happening now.

Use *was* and *were* when talking about things that have already happened.

Use *is* and *was* when talking about one person, place, thing, or animal.

Use *are* and *were* when talking about more than one person, place, thing, or animal and with the word *you*.

> **I <u>am</u> six years old.** > **You <u>are</u> six years old.**

> **Jim <u>is</u> seven years old.** > **Last year Jim <u>was</u> six.**

> **Kate and Nate <u>are</u> eight.** > **They <u>were</u> seven last year.**

8. Do not use the word *ain't* or spell verbs incorrectly as they are often mispronounced.

> **We <u>ain't</u> going.** → **We <u>are not</u> going.**

> **We <u>wanna</u> leave.** → **We <u>want to</u> leave.**

> **Are you <u>gonna</u> go?** → **Are you <u>going to</u> go?**

> **<u>Dontcha</u> like her?** → **<u>Don't you</u> like her?**

were leaving for detroit

michigan at 800

We're leaving for Detroit,

Michigan at 8:00

we red the book the three

pigs on friday

We read the book.

The Three

Pigs on Friday.

we dont have they're
gift ready yet

We dont have they're

gift ready yet!

---

the other day rod look
at bobs knew car

The other day rod looked at

Bobs knew car.

was those to boy's in the halloween parade

Were
Was those to boy's in the
Halloween parade?

we wanna go two joes house on thursday

We wanna go to Joes
house on Thursday.

the weekend days is friday saturday and sunday

The weekend days are Friday, Saturday, and a Sunday.

there going two the movie on friday knight

Their going to the movie on Friday Knight.

Name: _____ Date: _____ Unit 2 - 9

I read

i red the book green eggs

and ham by dr. seuss.

I read the book Green eggs

and Ham by Dr. Seuss.

Name: _____ Date: _____ Unit 2 - 10

W   do not   have

we aint got any gas

left in the car.

We do not have any gas

left in the car.

Name: _I'm_____ Date: _____ (Unit 2 - 11)

_I am_

going   _to_   _to_   _P_
im gonna go two pine

_S_   _to_   _see_   _J_
street too sea jake.

I am going to Pine Street to

see Jake.

Name: _____ Date: _____ (Unit 2 - 12)

_We_   _hear_
us can here the bells

_S_
at 1000 on sunday.

We can hear the bells at

10:00 on Sunday.

M   She
mom said her already
   washed
wash~~ed~~ all of the dishs

Mom said she already

washed all of the dishs.

                    dishes.

they   aren't
them aint being very
          to
nice too the girl's.

they aren't being very

nice to the girls.

do you wanna here
jane sing a song.

want to hear

Do you want to hear

Jane sing a song?

Max and I

me and max is gonna
get candy on halloween.

Max and I

Me and Max are going to

get candy on Halloween.

Name: _____ Date: _____ Unit 2 - 17

Do you

dontcha like candy!

gum or popcorn.?

Do you like candy!

gum, or popcorn?

Name: _____ Date: _____ Unit 2 - 18

their is a trip in october

two madison wisconsin.

There

Their is a trip in October

to Madison, Wisconsin.

Name: _____ Date: _____ (Unit 2 - 19)

Y
yesterday at 6:00 u.s ~we~

walk~ed~ *to* two tims party.

Yesterday at 6:00 we

walked to Tims party.

Name: __*H*__

December 8, 2009
Dec. 8, 2009   Date: ~2009~   (Unit 2 - 20)
12/8/09

*I*s halloween on
O
october 31 *in* 2004. *no*

Is Halloween on

October 31, in 2004?

Unit 2 — Assessment

Name: Christiana   Date: 1/15/09

1. i red the book green eggs and ham by dr. seuss.

(editing marks: read, capital I, capital G, capital E, capital S, capital D)

2. yesterday at 6:00 we walked two tim's party.

(editing marks: capital Y, to, capital T)

3. was those to boy's in the halloween parade.

(editing marks: Were, two, capital H)

Score all words, group of numbers, or punctuation marks in these sentences as one point each, whether or not a correction is needed.

Score: _____ /34 _____ %

Unit 2 — Assessment

Answer Key

I read   G

1. i red the book green

E   H   D

eggs and ham by dr.

S

seuss.

Y

2. yesterday at 6:00 we

to T

walked two tim's party.

Were   two boys

3. was those to boy's in the

H

halloween parade?

1. We're leaving for Detroit, Michigan at 8:00.

2. We read the book <u>The Three Pigs</u> on Friday.

3. We don't have their gift ready yet.

4. The other day Rod looked at Bob's new car.

5. Were those two boys in the Halloween parade?***

6. We want to go to Joe's house on Thursday.

7. The weekend days are Friday, Saturday, and Sunday.

8. They're going to the movie on Friday night.

9. I read the book <u>Green Eggs and Ham</u> by Dr. Seuss.***

10. We don't have any gas left!

11. I'm going to go to Pine Street to see Jake.

12. We can hear the bells at 10:00 on Sunday.

13. Mom said, "She already washed all the dishes."

14. They aren't being very nice to the girls!

15. Do you want to hear Jane sing a song?

16. Max and I are going to get candy on Halloween.

17. Don't you like candy, gum, or popcorn?

18. There is a trip in October to Madison, Wisconsin.

19. Yesterday at 6:00 we walked to Tim's party.***

20. Is Halloween on October 31, 2004?

*** *Unit 2 Assessment answers*

Unit 3
Rules to Know

1. Capitalize a relationship word used in place of a name if no word is used before it such as *my*, *your*, *their*, etc. To help determine if the relationship word should be capitalized, try substituting a name for the word. If the sentence makes sense, the word is being used in place of a name and should be capitalized.

   ➤ **Did Dad want to go with us? My dad wants to go with us.**
   ➤ **He thought Mom was nice. Your mom is nice.**

2. A quotation shows the speaker's exact words. Use quotation marks at the beginning and ending of a quotation to show where the speaker started and stopped talking. Begin a quotation with a capital letter. When writing a quotation, put the punctuation marks inside the quotation marks.

   ➤ **"Today we are going to the zoo," said Bill.**
   ➤ **Mary asked, "Can we go with you?"**

3. Use the correct punctuation to separate a quotation from the rest of the sentence. In a telling sentence use a comma between the quotation and the sentence and end the sentence with a period.

   ➤ **Dad said, "It is raining."**
   ➤ **"It is raining," said Dad.**

4. In an asking sentence, use a question mark after the quotation. If the quotation is before the speaker's name, put a period at the end of the sentence. If the speaker's name is before the quotation, separate the quotation with a comma.

   ➤ **"Where are we going?" asked Jane.**
   ➤ **Jane asked, "Where are we going?"**

5. In an exclamation, use an exclamation mark after the quotation. If the quotation is before the speaker's name, put a period at the end of the sentence. If the speaker's name is before the quotation, separate the quotation with a comma.

   ➤ **"That house is on fire!" shouted the man.**
   ➤ **The man shouted, "That house is on fire!"**

6. To form the plural possessive of a plural noun that ends in *s*, add only an apostrophe. If the plural noun does not end in *s*, add an apostrophe and an *s* ('s).

> ➣ **His two brothers' bikes were blue.**
> ➣ **The new children's library section is nice.**

7. The past tense of some verbs is made by changing the spelling.

> ➣ **Last week my dog <u>ran</u> away.**   (run)
> ➣ **We <u>bought</u> some milk at the store.**   (buy)
> ➣ **He <u>drew</u> a picture in art class.**   (draw)

8. A present tense verb shows something is happening now. Add *s* or *es* to most verbs if the subject is one person, place, thing, or animal. Do not add *s* or *es* to a verb if the subject is *I* or *you* or if it means more than one. The ending *–ing* is also added to make present tense verbs.

> ➣ **She cooks supper.**   ➣ **He likes to swim.**
> ➣ **They cook supper.**   ➣ **The boys like to swim.**
> ➣ **I cook supper.**   ➣ **You like to swim.**
> ➣ **I am cooking supper.**   ➣ **They are eating supper.**

9. Use *doesn't* with singular nouns meaning one person, place, thing, or animal. Use *don't* with plural nouns meaning more than one person, place, thing, or animal and with *I*, *you*, *we*, and *they*.

> ➣ **Joe <u>doesn't</u> like to play tag.**
> ➣ **That dog <u>doesn't</u> belong to me.**
> ➣ **I <u>don't</u> think he is ready yet.**
> ➣ **The new kittens <u>don't</u> have names.**

10. Some nouns change their spelling instead of adding *s* or *es* to mean more than one. A few nouns can mean either one or more than one with the same spelling. Examples of these irregular plural nouns are as follows:

> **man / men**   **woman / women**
> **child / children**   **mouse / mice**
> **foot / feet**   **tooth / teeth**
> **sheep / sheep**   **deer / deer**

pat asked is the three cats
names spot fluffy and tiger?

Pat asked" Are the three cats
names Spot Fluffy and Tiger?"

my dad has the book how
to play golf" said robert.

"My dad has the book How
to Play Golf," said Robert.

D   G

did grandma go too missouri

on november 1, 2004?

Did grandma go to Misouri

on November 1, 2004?

We Her and I   rode   M

me and her rided megans

bike and fell off.

Her and I   rode Megans

bike and fell off.

1/27

B
"
bob said, yesterday us play ed
We
                                                                        "
with the gooses at the farm.
geese

Bob said "yesterday we played
with thegese at the farm."

M   I   aren't going to
mr. Oh and i ain't gonna
here   It
come hear on tuesday.

Mr. Oh and I aren't going to
comehere on Tuesday.

/27

Doesn'ts

dont sue plays the organ at

two
too churchs every sunday?
S

Doesn't Sue play the organ at

two churchs every Sunday?

"I
i works on thanksgiving

until 4:00" said dad.

"I work on Thanksgiving

until 4:00 "said dad.

Name: _____   Date: _____   Unit 3 - 9

M'   went
my mom goed with
                    s   to   see
dad and sally two sea
the house.

My   mom   went   with

dad   and   Sally   to   see

the   house.

Name: _____   Date: _____   Unit 3 - 10

" His   all
him too brothers rooms
were   I
was messy i said.

"His   two   brothers   rooms

were   messy."   I   said.

There
"they're goes to no mice mouses and
three rats, screamed ben!

"there goes two mice and
three rat's screaned Ben!

A we two
at the farm us saw too
horse's and three sheeps.

At the farm we saw two
horse's and three sheep.

Name: _____ Date: _____ Unit 3 - 13

dr gates and him wife
lives in mexico.

Dr. Gates and his wife

live in Mexico.

Name: _____ Date: _____ Unit 3 - 14

home house

"bills grandparents house
is really big" said molly.

"Bills grandparents house

is really big" said Molly.

too womans and for

mans runned for mayor

too woman and four

men rane for mayor.

tims little sister lost too

tooth, said aunt kathy.

"Tims little sister lost two

teath "said aunt Kathy.

mark said there mom drived
us too school on monday

grandpa" asked wood you
help me" wash dishs?

Grandpa" asked will you help
me" wash the dishs

they're was for deers in the woulds buy my house

There where four deer in the wood's by my house.

watch out four those branchs kim shouted

"Watch out for those branchs Kim" shouted.

Unit 3 — Assessment

Name: _____ Date: _____

1. pat asked is the three cats names spot fluffy and tiger

2. dr gates and him wife lives in mexico

3. tims little sister lost too tooths said aunt kathy.

Score all words, group of numbers, or punctuation marks in these sentences as one point each, whether or not a correction is needed.

Score: _____ /41 _____ **%**

Unit 3 — Assessment

Answer Key

    P   Are

1. pat asked, "is the three

              S   F

   cats' names spot, fluffy,

        T

   and tiger?"

    D G   his

2. dr. gates and him wife

          M

   lives in mexico.

   T   two

3. "tim's little sister lost too

   teeth   A   K

   tooths," said aunt kathy.

Unit 3
Answer Key

1. Pat asked, "Are the three cats' names Spot, Fluffy, and Tiger?***

2. "My dad has the book <u>How to Play Golf</u>," said Robert.

3. Did Grandma go to Missouri on November 1, 2004?

4. She and I rode Megan's bike and fell off!

5. Bob said, "Yesterday we played with the geese at the farm."

6. Mr. Oh and I aren't coming here on Tuesday.

7. Doesn't Sue play the organ at two churches every Sunday?

8. "I work on Thanksgiving until 4:00," said Dad.

9. My mom went with Dad and Sally to see the house.

10. "His two brothers' rooms were messy," I said.

11. "There goes two mice and three rats!" screamed Ben.

12. At the farm we saw two horses and three sheep.

13. Dr. Gates and his wife live in Mexico.***

14. "Bill's grandparents' house is really big," said Molly.

15. Two women and four men ran for mayor.

16. "Tim's little sister lost two teeth, " said Aunt Kathy.***

17. Mark said, "Their mom drove us to school on Monday."

18. Grandpa asked, "Would you help me wash dishes?"

19. There were four deer in the woods by my house.

20. "Watch out for those branches!" Kim shouted.

***Unit 3 Assessment answers**

Unit 4
Rules to Know

1. A friendly letter has five parts: heading, greeting, body, closing, and signature. The heading contains the sender's address and the date. When writing an address, capitalize the names of streets, cities, and states. Write the street address on a separate line from the city and state. Capitalize an abbreviation for any type of street or road and put a period after it. Put a comma between the city and the state. Capitalize both letters in the state abbreviation, but do not put a period after it. Put a comma in the date between the day and the year.

> **9684 Sunset Rd.**
> **Des Moines, IA 50321**
> **December 5, 2004**

[handwritten: 4030 Monovale Crossing Cumming, GA 30041 March 16, 2009]

2. Capitalize the first word of the greeting in a letter. Put a comma after the greeting in a friendly letter.

> **Dear Bob,**   > **Hello Jill,**

3. Capitalize the first word of the closing in a letter and put a comma after it.

> **Your friend,**   > **Love always,**

4. Indent the first word of the body of a friendly letter by moving the first word a little to the right. When writing the closing and signature in a friendly letter, move them to the right to line up with the heading of the letter.

> 　　　　　　　　　　**2233 Holly Ave.**
> 　　　　　　　　　　**Arcadia, CA 91007**
> 　　　　　　　　　　**May 5, 2005**
> **Dear Bob,**
> 　　**How are you? Did you get a new bike on Saturday?**
> 　　　　　　　　　　**Your friend,**
> 　　　　　　　　　　**Jon**

5. When writing an address, follow all the same rules as in the address of a heading, as well as capitalizing names and titles.

> **Mr. Joe Ross**
> **16 Maple St.**
> **Minneapolis, MN 55382**

6. A negative is a word like *no*, *not*, *none*, or *never*. A contraction with the word *not* is also a negative. Do not use two negatives together in a sentence.

> He doesn't have no money.　→　He doesn't have any money.
> She never had no lunch.　→　She never had any lunch.
> Can't you see nothing?　→　Can't you see anything?

7. The subject of a sentence tells who the sentence is about. A noun or a pronoun can be the subject of a sentence. Do not use both a noun and a pronoun to mean the same person or thing in a sentence.

> The girl she went skating.　→　The girl went skating.
> Tom he came to my house.　→　Tom came to my house.
> Jill and I we like to play.　→　Jill and I like to play.

8. Be careful not to confuse these words: *are/our*, *you're/your*, *it's/its*.

- *are* is a verb
- *our* means something belongs to us
- *you're* is a contraction for "you are"
- *your* is a pronoun that shows ownership
- *it's* is a contraction for "it is" or "it has" (*Use an apostrophe in a contraction.*)
- *its* is a possessive pronoun that shows ownership (*Do not use an apostrophe.*)

> Are you coming to our house today?
> You're the youngest member of your family.
> It's time to give the dog its bath.
> It's been a long time since I have seen you.

3/16

"Our   Our
are friends will come too are

       F
house on friday," said dad.

"Our friends will come to our
house on Friday," said dad.

C   B
cory bennett

47 highview ave
O   CA
oakland, ca   93740

Cory Bennett

47 Highview Ave
Oakland, CA   93740

D   S
did we read the book santas

    E   W
busy elves on wednesday?

Did we read the book Santas

Busy Elves on Wednesday?

Name: Christana _____ Date: 3/16/09 Unit 4 - 4

Mrs. Green and I like to go

shoping

me and mrs green we

likes too go shopping

Mrs. Green and I like to go

Shoping.

Name: _____ Date: _____ Unit 4 - 5

"I C D
is christmas on december
25, 2004 asked alissa?

"Is Christmas on December
25, 2004" asked Alissa?

Name: _____ Date: _____ Unit 4 - 6

I don't any
"i doesnt have no more
wrapping paper "said mom.

"I don't have any more
wrapping paper," said mom.

Name: _____ Date: _____ Unit 4 - 7

uncle dan he owns to
ranchs in texas.

Uncle Dan owns two
ranchs in Texas.

Name: _____ Date: _____ Unit 4 - 8

i wants too put lots of boxs
under the christmas tree.

I want to put lots of boxes
under the Christmas tree.

3/18

there dogs names is roxy
snickers and peanut.

There dogs names are Roxy
Snickers and Peanut.

santa claus he will bee hear
soon "said the excited elf

"Santa Claus will be hear
soon "said the excited elf.

206 pine street
akron oh 58903

december 11, 2004

dear amy.

i hope you can come too

are house for christmas

you're friend,

jan

206 Pine Street

Akron OH, 58903

December 11, 2004

Dear Amy,

I hope you can come to our

house for Christmas.

You're friend

Jan

For Christmas

four christmas i wants
candy toys and a bike.

For Christmas I want

candy, toys, and a bike.

i cant wait no longer four

santa claus two come

I cant wait any longer

for Santa Claus to come.

its almost time too feed

the cat it's food said seth.

"It's almost time to feed
the cat its food" said Seth.

scott smith

12 north road

billings mt 87651

Scott Smith

12 North Road

Billings, MT 87651

merry christmas everybody shouted "bobs little sister.

"Merry Christmas everybody!" shouted "Bobs little sister.

are foots will get cold if us stay out hear to long.

Our feet will get cold if we stay out hear to long.

here

Name: _____ Date: _____ Unit 4 - 18

He   bot
him buyed me and my
                New
sister a knew computer
         C
for christmas.

He bot me and my

sister a knew computer

for Christmas.

Name: _____ Date: _____ Unit 4 - 19

I   C
"the christmas party starts
              M   H
at 600 "said miss henry.

"The Christmas Party Starts

at 6:00 "said Miss Henry.

4731 west dr*W*i*ve*
*D*duluth m*MN*n 56035
*D*december 20, 2004
dear aunt *J*jill,
thank you f*for*our the gift.
your a nice aunt.
with love,
*J*jack

4731 West Drive
Duluth M.N. 56035
December 20, 2004
Dear aunt Jill,
Thank you for the gift.
Your a nice aunt.
With Love,
JaCK

Unit 4 — Assessment

Name: 100%   Date: 4/1

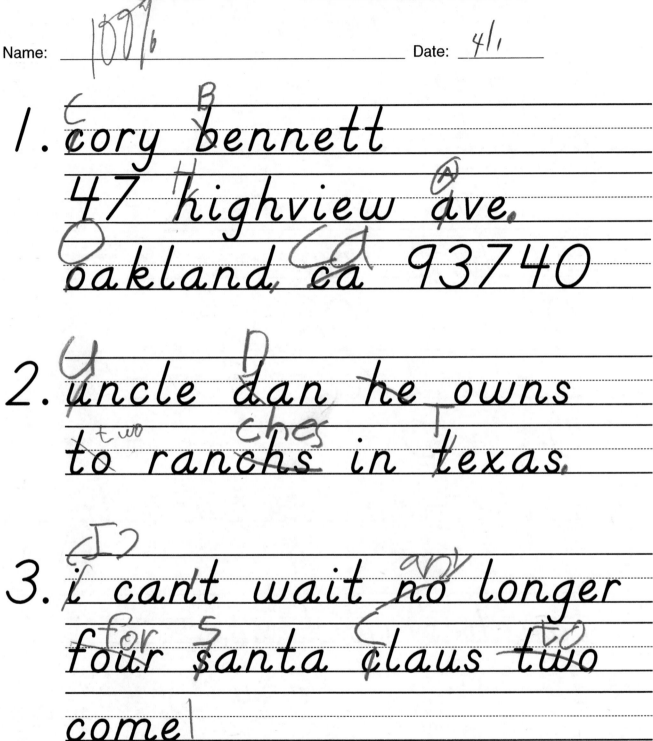

1. cory bennett
   47 highview ave.
   oakland, ca 93740

2. uncle dan he owns
   to ranchs in texas.

3. i cant wait no longer
   four santa claus two
   come!

Score all words, group of numbers, or punctuation marks in these sentences as one point each, whether or not a correction is needed.

Score: _____ /31 _____%

Unit 4 — Assessment

Answer Key

    C   B

1. cory bennett

    H   A

   47 highview ave.

   O   CA

   oakland, ca   93740

   U   D   two

2. uncle dan he owns to

                 T

   ranches in texas.

   I   any

3. i can't wait no longer

   for S   C   to

   four santa claus two come!

Unit 4

Answer Key

1. "Our friends will come to our house on Friday," said Dad.
2. Cory Bennett***
   47 Highview Ave.
   Oakland, CA 93740
3. Did we read the book <u>Santa's Busy Elves</u> on Wednesday?
4. Mrs. Green and I like to go shopping.
5. "Is Christmas on December 25, 2004?" asked Alissa.
6. "I don't have any more wrapping paper," said Mom.
7. Uncle Dan owns two ranches in Texas.***
8. I want to put lots of boxes under the Christmas tree.
9. Their dogs' names are Roxy, Snickers, and Peanut.
10. "Santa Claus will be here soon!" said the excited elf.
11.   206 Pine Street
             Akron, OH 58903
             December 11, 2004 (*can correct to reflect current date*)
    Dear Amy,
       I hope you can come to our house for Christmas.
                Your friend,
                Jan
12. For Christmas I want candy, toys, and a bike.
13. I can't wait any longer for Santa Claus to come.***
14. "It's almost time to feed the cat its food," said Seth.
15. Scott Smith
    12 North Road
    Billings, MT 87651
16. "Merry Christmas everybody!" shouted Bob's little sister.
17. Our feet will get cold if we stay out here too long.
18. He bought my sister and me a new computer for Christmas.
19. "The Christmas party starts at 6:00," said Miss Henry.
20.   4731 West Dr.
             Duluth, MN 56035
             December 20, 2004 (*can correct to reflect current date*)
    Dear Aunt Jill,
       Thank you for the gift. You're a nice aunt.
                With love,
                Jack

*** Unit 4 Assessment answers

Unit 5
Rules to Know

1. Use *a* and *an* before singular nouns (words meaning one person, place, thing, or animal). Use *a* before words that begin with a consonant sound. Use *an* before words beginning with a vowel or vowel sound.

   ➢ He had **a** bowl of cereal for breakfast.
   ➢ She had **an** egg for breakfast.
   ➢ She ate **an** hour before he did.

2. Use the helping verb *has* with one subject. Use the helping verb *have* with more than one subject and with the words *I* and *you*.

   ➢ The dog **has** a bone. (one subject)
   ➢ The boys **have** the ball. (more than one subject)
   ➢ I **have** a sister.
   ➢ You **have** a brother.

3. A *run-on sentence* has two complete thoughts that run into each other. Run-on sentences can be corrected by separating the thoughts. If the ideas in the two parts have nothing in common, separate them into two sentences with a period.

   ➢ Today it is rainy tomorrow is Saturday. (incorrect)
   ➢ Today it is rainy. Tomorrow is Saturday. (correct)

4. If the two ideas in a run-on sentence go together by having something in common, make a compound sentence out of the two thoughts. A compound sentence is made by combining two short sentences into one longer one. The two sentences are joined with a comma and a connecting word such as *and*, *but*, *yet*, or *while*.

   ➢ The girls go to West School their favorite subject is math. (incorrect)
   ➢ The girls go to West School, **and** their favorite subject is math. (correct)
   ➢ The boys wanted to play ball they couldn't find the field. (incorrect)
   ➢ The boys wanted to play ball, **but** they couldn't find the field. (correct)

W   N   Y
was new years day on

january 1, 2005?

Was New Years day on

January 1, 2005?

N   E
nicole evans

          S   B   S
1632 s. bridge st.

M   WI
madison, wi 64302

Nicole Evans

1632 S. Bridge St.

Madison, WI 64302

Name: _____ Date: 4 8 _____

For C

four christmas me got

I

toys, candy, and an

new

knew computer.

For Christmas I got

toys, candy, and a new

computer.

Name: _____ Date: _____

We went   For

us goed to florida four

I   A

vacation and me visit ann.

We went to Florida for

vacation and I visited

Ann.

~~Do~~

do you ~~has~~ have an apple or

~~a~~ an banana in ~~you're~~ your lunch?

Do you have an apple or
a banana in your
lunch?

i like gifts christmas

is my favorite holiday.

I like gifts. Christmas
is my favorite Holiday.

its been about a hour since all the bus left.

(an)
(es)

Its been about an hour
since all the buses left.

He   bought

him buyed the book, the smallest snowman, for we.

He bught the book, The
Smallest Snowman, for us.

It's

its sunny outside today

                                                was
but yesterday it ~~were~~ to

snowy.

Its sunny outside today,
but yesterday it was to
snowy.

Mrs. O   are
mrs ott and mom they

is good friend's

Mrs. Ott and mom are
good friends.

50 king boulevard

boston, ma 07249

january 11 2005

dear uncle harry,

your lucky too live in nevada its to cold hear,

you're nephew

mike

50 King Boulevard

Boston MA 07249

January 11, 2005

dear Uncle Harry,

your lucky to live in Nevada its to cold here

your nephew,

Mike

B
bens sister shouted,

don't   any
dont do that no more.

Bens sister shouted

dont do that any morl

A   men
all the mans and boy's

were   to
was first two line up.

All the men and boys

were first to line up.

both girls dresses was knew,
~~was~~ **were**

and they was very pretty.
~~was~~ **were**

Both girls dresses were knew, and
they were very pretty.

my sisters friend she is
My ~~she~~

coming over at 300
3:00

My sisters friend is

coming over at 3:00.

~~The~~
the snow is melting, and
spring will ~~bee~~ _be_ hear soon.

The snow is melting, and
spring will be hear soon.

~~Me~~
me and him ~~we~~ never
~~has~~ _have_ no fun ~~they're~~ _they're_.

Me and him never
have fun they're.

#4

Didn't

have   for
didnt you has a egg four
breakfast, asked karen.

"Didnt you have a egg for

breakfast? /asked karen.

Will   snow   four
will it snows three, for
or five inchs on
thursday?

Will it snow three, four,

or five, inchs on

thursday?

Unit 5 — Assessment

Answer Key

D   have

1. ~~do~~ you ~~has~~ an apple or ~~an~~

                  your

banana in ~~you're~~ lunch?

  T

2. ~~the~~ snow is melting, and

                  here

spring will ~~bee~~ ~~hear~~ soon.

  I

3. ~~it's~~ sunny outside today,

                  was

but yesterday it ~~were~~ too

snowy.

Unit 5
Answer Key

1. Was New Year's Day on January 1, 2005?

2. Nicole Evans

   1632 S. Bridge St.

   Madison, WI 64302

3. For Christmas I got toys, candy, and a new computer.

4. We went to Florida for vacation, and I visited Ann.

5. Do you have an apple or a banana in your lunch?***

6. I like gifts. Christmas is my favorite holiday.

7. It's been about an hour since all the buses left.

8. He bought the book <u>The Smallest Snowman</u> for us.

9. It's sunny outside today, but yesterday it was too snowy.***

10. Mrs. Ott and Mom are good friends.

11.   50 King Boulevard

          Boston, MA 07249

          January 11, 2005 (*can correct to reflect current date*)

    Dear Uncle Harry,

       You're lucky to live in Nevada. It's too cold here.

          Your nephew,

          Mike

12. Ben's sister shouted, "Don't do that anymore!"

13. All the men and boys were first to line up.

14. Both girls' dresses were new, and they were very pretty.

15. My sister's friend is coming over at 3:00.

16. The snow is melting, and spring will be here soon.***

17. He and I never have any fun there.

18. "Didn't you have an egg for breakfast?" asked Karen.

19. Will it snow three, four, or five inches on Thursday?

20.   123 Oak Street

          Atlanta, GA 47329

          January 20, 2005 (*can correct to reflect current date*)

    Dear Katlin,

       We're having fun in Hawaii on our vacation!

          Your friend,

          Megan

*** Unit 5 Assessment answers

Unit 6
Rules to Know

1. Use a comma after *yes* or *no* at the beginning of a sentence when the word begins to answer a question.

   ➤ **Are you Jan's sister?**   → **Yes, I am her sister.**
   ➤ **Do you go to Valley School?**   → **No, I go to Lake School.**

2. An *adjective* is a word that describes a noun or a pronoun. Add *er* to most adjectives to compare two people, places, things, or animals. Add *est* to compare more than two.

   tall   boy

   ➤ **He is tall<u>er</u> than his brother.**
   ➤ **He is the tall<u>est</u> of all three children.**

3. Nouns that end in the letter *y* have special rules for making plurals. If the word ends with a vowel followed by *y*, just add *s*. If the word ends with a consonant followed by *y*, change the *y* to *i* and add *es*.

   ➤ **I lost my <u>keys</u> yesterday. (key)**
   ➤ **She had three birthday <u>parties</u>. (party)**   *ies*

4. Nouns that end in the letter *f* or *fe* also have a special rule for making plurals. In most words change the *f* to *v* and add *es*.

   ➤ **calf**   → **calves**
   ➤ **shelf**   → **shelves**
   ➤ **knife**   → **knives**

5. *Helping verbs* are sometimes used with main action verbs. Some examples of helping verbs are *has*, *have*, *had*, *is*, *are*, *was*, *were*, and *will*. The words saw and seen tell about something in the past. Use *saw* without a helping verb, and use *seen* with a helping verb.

   ➤ **Yesterday I <u>saw</u> you at the mall.**
   ➤ **I <u>have seen</u> you there before.**

is groundhogs day on
february 2 2005.

Is Ground Hog day on
February 2, 2005?

brandon beck
15 spring drive
baltimore md 13579

Brandon Beck
15 Spring Drive
Baltimore, MD 13579

We
P
us celebrates presidents

D
day on the third

F
monday in february.

We celebrate Presidents

Day on the third

Monday in February.

What's Aren't
B
Mr
mr berry said, "isn't you

any
giving no valentine's?"

yes i has the book to many pancakes.
(Y) (I. have) (Too many)

Yes I have the book To
Many Pancakes.

He four
him made for shelfs
and they was nice.
(Were)

He made four shelfs
and they were nice.

Jake   I

me and jake we is the

fastest   are

faster runners on the team.

Jake and I are the

fastest runners on the team.

Yes   two

yes the too puppys

rane

runned away.

Yes, the two puppys

ran away.

"Your

you're brothers class
starts at 2:00," said mom.

"Your brothers class
starts at 2:00," said mom.

We're going   to
were gonna go two
6
grandmas house and
We'll
well have fun.

We're going to
Grandmas house and
we'll have fun.

99 hemlock st

flint mi 56783

february 11, 2005

dear jenny

can you come over on
saturday its my birthday

you're friend,

sandy

99 Hemlock St.

Flint, MI. 56783

February 11, 2005

Dear Jenny,

Can you come over on
Saturday. Its my birthday.

Your Friend,

Christian

Mrs. B H

miss brown said happy valentines day everyone

"Mrs. Brown said "Happy Valentines Day everyone!"

my larger

yes are family is largest than you're family

Yes, my family is larger than your family.

mom said never play
with no knifes.

Mom said, "Never Play
with Knives."

yesterday grandpa he drived
us too school, said todd.

Yesterday grandpa drove
us to school," said Todd.

Name: _____ Date: _____ 5/1 5/1 (Unit 6 - 16)

In
in are garden us has we have
flowers and bushs.

In our garden we have
flowers and bushes.

Name: _____ Date: _____ (Unit 6 - 17)

I saw ponies
yes, i seen lots of ponys
at the farm.

Yes, I saw lots of ponies
at the farm.

~~All~~ Children

all the childs went out

to   an

~~two~~ play for ~~a~~ hour

All the children went out

to play for an hour.

She

an

~~her~~ had ~~a~~ orange, a apple,

for

and a pear ~~four~~ a snack.

She had an orange, apple,

and a pear for snack.

1103 north st

fargo, nd 73920

february 20, 2005

dear grandma,

 its coldest hear than in

florida im ready for spring

with love,

julie

1103 North st.

Fargo, ND 73920

February 20, 2005

Dear Grandma,

It's colder here than florida

I'm ready for spring

With Love,

Julie

Unit 6 — Assessment

Name: _____ Date: _____

1. him made for shelfs
   and they was nice

2. yes the too puppys
   runned away

3. yes are family is
   largest than you're
   family

Score all words, group of numbers, or punctuation marks in these sentences as one point each, whether or not a correction is needed.

Score: _____ /28 _____ %

Unit 6 — Assessment

Answer Key

He   four shelves

1. ~~him~~ made for ~~shelfs~~,

were

and they ~~was~~ nice.

Y   two puppies

2. ~~yes~~, the ~~too puppys~~

ran

~~runned~~ away.

Y our   larger

3. ~~yes~~, ~~are~~ family is ~~largest~~

your

than ~~you're~~ family.

Unit 6
Answer Key

1. Is Groundhog's Day on February 2, 2005? (*can correct to reflect current date*)
2. Brandon Beck
   15 Spring Drive
   Baltimore, MD 13579
3. We celebrate Presidents' Day on the third Monday in February.
4. Mr. Berry said, "Aren't you giving any valentines?"
5. Yes, I have the book <u>Too Many Pancakes</u>.
6. He made four shelves, and they were nice.***
7. Jake and I are the fastest runners on the team!
8. Yes, the two puppies ran away.***
9. "Your brother's class starts at 2:00," said Mom
10. We're going to go to grandma's house, and we'll have fun!
11.   99 Hemlock St.
         Flint, MI 56783
         February 11, 2005 (*can correct to reflect current date*)
    Dear Jenny,
      Can you come over on Saturday? It's my birthday!
         Your friend,
         Sandy
12. Miss Brown said, "Happy Valentine's Day everyone!"
13. Yes, our family is larger than your family.***
14. Mom said, "Never play with any knives."
15. "Yesterday Grandpa drove us to school," said Todd.
16. In our garden we have flowers and bushes.
17. Yes, I saw lots of ponies at the farm.
18. All the children went out to play for an hour.
19. She had an orange, an apple, and a pear for a snack.
20.   1103 North St.
         Fargo, ND 73920
         February 20, 2005 (*can correct to reflect current date*)
    Dear Grandma,
      It's colder here than in Florida. I'm ready for spring!
         With love,
         Julie

*** Unit 6 Assessment answers

it warms up in march and the snow begins too melt

mark troy
427 highway c
des moines ia 53702

is st patricks day in
march or april he asked

him taked us skating
at 1000 last sunday

dad he is the goodest driver i no

you ain't never gonna find my gold laughed the leprechaun

yes i likes the play we

seen last friday knight

i likes mouses four pets

but mom want an cat

mr o'reilly shouted
happy st patricks day

i cant wait four spring
my birthday comes in
march

27 hill drive

denver co 83726

march 11 2005

dear uncle buck

im glad that ill get to

visit you're too ranchs

you're nephew

rick

yesterday my sister and me eated a egg for breakfast

the boy he peted calfs sheeps and goats

are house it ain't on
elm street said david

am i tallest or shortest
than you asked kim

is it snowed right now
asked grandma

yesterday we red the book
the silly shamrock

yes are dad is runing in the mens marathon

her seen too tiger for monkey and an lion at the zoo

500 meadow road

burlington vt 05114

march 20 2005

dear grandma

thanks for takeing me two

the zoo it was great

with love

nikki

Unit 7 — Assessment

Name: _____ Date: _____

1. yes i likes the play
we seen last friday
knight

2. yesterday my sister
and me eated a egg
for breakfast

3. am i tallest or
shortest than you
asked kim

Score all words, group of numbers, or punctuation marks in these sentences as one point each, whether or not a correction is needed.

Score: _____/36 _____%

Unit 7 — Assessment
Answer Key

Y   I liked

1. ~~yes, i likes~~ the play we

   saw   F

   ~~seen last friday knight.~~

   Y

2. ~~yesterday~~ my sister and

   I ate an

   ~~me eated a egg~~ for

   ~~breakfast.~~

   A   I taller   shorter

3. ~~"am i tallest or shortest~~

                     K

   ~~than you?" asked kim.~~

Unit 7

Answer Key

1. It starts to warm up in March, and the snow begins to melt.
2. Mark Troy
   427 Highway C
   Des Moines, IA 53702
3. "Is St. Patrick's Day in March or April?" he asked.
4. He took us skating at 10:00 last Sunday.
5. Dad is the best driver I know.
6. "You aren't ever going to find my gold!" laughed the leprechaun.
7. Yes, I liked the play we saw last Friday night.***
8. I like mice for pets, but Mom wants a cat.
9. Mr. O'Reilly shouted, "Happy St. Patrick's Day!"
10. I can't wait for spring. My birthday comes in March.
11.   27 Hill Drive
         Denver, CO 83726
         March 11, 2005 (*can correct to reflect current date*)
    Dear Uncle Buck,
       I'm glad I'll get to visit your two ranches.
              Your nephew,
              Rick
12. Yesterday my sister and I ate an egg for breakfast.***
13. The boy petted calves, sheep, and goats.
14. "Our house isn't on Elm Street," said David.
15. "Am I taller or shorter than you?" asked Kim.***
16. "Is it snowing right now?" asked Grandma.
17. Yesterday we read the book <u>The Silly Shamrock</u>.
18. Yes, our dad is running in the men's marathon.
19. She saw two tigers, four monkeys, and a lion at the zoo.
20.   500 Meadow Road
         Burlington, VT 05114
         March 20, 2005 (*can correct to reflect current date*)
    Dear Grandma,
       Thanks for taking me to the zoo. It was great!
              With love,
              Nikki

*** Unit 7 Assessment answers

Name: ______________________ Date: ____________ Unit 8 - 1

knew leafs are comeing
out on the trees said mrs
wood

Name: ______________________ Date: ____________ Unit 8 - 2

mr jake hall
100 apple circle
atlanta ga 26721

have you saw a spring
robin yet asked mary
beth

should the boys team or
girls team go first

her red the book

springtime too us tuesday

yes they help me and

amy paint are room

last weak

for easter i want
candy toys and a egg

your the nicer friend
of all said eric

happy easter everyone
shouted the easter
bunny

we wants two play
outside but its raining

508 country blvd

memphis tn 43797

april 11 2005

dear aunt mary

thanks four the too

easter dress there so nice

much love

abi

pat and mom seen for

mooses in the woulds

we doesn't have no more

of are money left said

the boy's

john he rided him bike
two school today at 800

did you here that april
shower's bring may flower's

us has daisys and lilys
in are garden she said

my favorite sport are golf
mr owen is a great coach

miss cooper like two
study about wolfs

is dad to tired too
took us their i asked

933 pine ave

seattle wa 97601

april 20 2005

dear bill

i havent saw you four a

long time whats knew

your cousin

peter

Unit 8 — Assessment

Name: _____ Date: _____

1. 508 country blvd

memphis tn 43797

april 11 2005

dear aunt mary

thanks four the too

easter dress there so

nice

much love

abi

Score all words, group of numbers, or punctuation marks in these sentences as one point each, whether or not a correction is needed.

Score: _____ /31 _____ %

Unit 8 — Assessment

Answer Key

1.
        C   B

508 country blvd.

    M   TN

memphis, tn 43797

    A

april 11, 2005

D   A   M

dear aunt mary,

   T   for

thanks four the

two E

too easter dresses.

They're

there so nice!

     M

much love,

   A

abi

1. "New leaves are coming out on the trees," said Mrs. Wood.
2. Mr. Jake Hall
   100 Apple Circle
   Atlanta, GA 26721
3. "Have you seen a spring robin yet?" asked Mary Beth.
4. Should the boys' team or girls' team go first?
5. She read the book <u>Springtime</u> to us Tuesday.
6. Yes, they helped Amy and me paint our room last week.
7. For Easter I want candy, toys, and an egg.
8. "You're the nicest friend of all," said Eric.
9. "Happy Easter everyone!" shouted the Easter Bunny.
10. We want to play outside, but it's raining.
11.   508 Country Blvd.***
       Memphis, TN 43797
       April 11, 2005 (*can correct to reflect current date*)
    Dear Aunt Mary,
       Thanks for the two Easter dresses. They're so nice!
          Much love,
          Abi
12. Pat and Mom saw four moose in the woods.
13. "We don't have any more of our money left," said the boys.
14. John rode his bike to school today at 8:00.
15. Did you hear that April showers bring May flowers?
16. "We have daisies and lilies in our garden," she said.
17. My favorite sport is golf. Mr. Owen is a great coach.
18. Miss Cooper likes to study about wolves.
19. "Is Dad too tired to take us there?" I asked.
20.   933 Pine Ave.
       Seattle, WA 97601
       April 20, 2005 (*can correct to reflect current date*)
    Dear Bill,
       I haven't seen you for a long time. What's new?
          Your cousin,
          Peter

*** Unit 8 Assessment answers

on saturday im gonna

go camping said al

miss kay peters

742 carson ave

madison wi 59304

its to nice out two stay inside said ray

us goed two the fair i love the roller coaster

me and bob is trying
too sell are for knew
puppys

remember two pack all
the lunchs four the trip

him goed too the beach
and swimmed

at the cabin us goed
fishing hikeing and
swimming

did mom or dad sea
brads knew bike i
asked

uncle max he don't get
the newspaper no more

2345 main st

dallas tx 76590

may 11 2005

dear grandpa

were leaving sunday four

you're house sea you soon

with love

matt

how many tooths has
you lost asked molly

i blowed the bigger
bubble of all shouted
nick

her check out the book
beach fun at the library

yes their will bee a
memorial day parade at
1000

i needs two by a
eggplant and to loafs
of bread

is memorial day on
may 31 2005

school is almost over
and summer will soon
bee hear

the students teacher said
have a nice vacation

40 south ave

trenton nj 08942

may 20 2005

dear mrs roads

ive enjoyed you're class

have a nice summer

your friend

andy

Unit 9 — Assessment

Name: _____ Date: _____

1. us goed two the fair i loved the roller coaster

2. at the cabin us goed fishing hikeing and swimming

3. i blowed the bigger bubble of all shouted nick

Score all words, group of numbers, or punctuation marks in these sentences as one point each, whether or not a correction is needed.

Score: _____ /37 _____%

Unit 9 — Assessment

Answer Key

1. $\overset{\text{We went to}}{\underline{\text{us goed two the fair.}}}$ $\overset{I}{\underline{i}}$

$\underline{\text{loved the roller coaster!}}$

2. $\overset{A}{\underline{\text{at the cabin us goed}}}$ $\overset{\text{we went}}{}$

$\overset{\text{hiking}}{\underline{\text{fishing, hikeing, and}}}$

$\underline{\text{swimming.}}$

3. $\overset{\text{I blew} \qquad \text{biggest}}{\underline{\text{"i blowed the bigger bubble}}}$

$\overset{N}{\underline{\text{of all!" shouted nick.}}}$

Unit 9
Answer Key

1. "On Saturday I'm going to go camping," said Al.
2. Miss Kay Peters
   742 Carson Ave.
   Madison, WI 59304
3. "It's too nice out to stay inside," said Ray.
4. We went to the fair. I loved the roller coaster!***
5. Bob and I are trying to sell our four new puppies.
6. Remember to pack all the lunches for the trip.
7. He went to the beach and swam.
8. At the cabin we went fishing, hiking, and swimming.***
9. "Did Mom or Dad see Brad's new bike?" I asked.
10. Uncle Max doesn't get the newspaper any more.
11.   2345 Main St.
           Dallas, TX 76590
           May 11, 2005 (*can correct to reflect current date*)
    Dear Grandpa,
      We're leaving Sunday for your house. See you soon!
           With love,
           Matt
12. "How many teeth have you lost?" asked Molly.
13. "I blew the biggest bubble of all!" shouted Nick.***
14. She checked out the book <u>Beach Fun</u> at the library.
15. Yes, there will be a Memorial Day parade at 10:00.
16. I need to buy an eggplant and two loaves of bread.
17. Is Memorial Day on May 31, 2005?
18. School is almost over, and summer will soon be here.
19. The students' teacher said, "Have a nice vacation!"
20.   40 South Ave.
           Trenton, NJ 08942
           May 20, 2005 (*can correct to reflect current date*)
    Dear Mrs. Roads,
      I've enjoyed your class. Have a nice summer!
           Your friend,
           Andy

*** ***Unit 9 Assessment answers***

Cumulative Assessment

Name : _____ Date: _____ Score: _____ /238

1. were leaving four detroit michigan at 800

(From page 36, #1)

2. mom said her already wash all the dishs

(From page 36, #13)

3. bills grandparents house is really big said molly

(From page 51, #14)

4. is christmas on december 25 2004 asked alissa

(From page 67, #5)

5. do you has a apple or an banana in you're lunch

(From page 82, #5)

Cumulative Assessment _(cont.)

6. cory bennett
   47 high ave
   oakland ca   93740
   (From page 67, #2)

7. my sisters friend is
   coming over at 300
   (From page 82, #15)

8. yes i has the book to
   many pancakes
   (From page 97, #5)

9. me and jake we is the
   faster runners on the
   team
   (From page 97, #7)

10. were gonna go two
    grandmas house and well
    have fun
    (From page 97, #10)

Cumulative Assessment (cont.)

11. yes i seen lots of ponys at the farm.

(From page 97, #17)

12. her seen too tiger for monkey and an lion at the zoo

(From page 111, #19)

13. i red the book green eggs and ham by dr seuss

(From page 36, #9)

14. uncle max he don't get the newspaper no more

(From page 139, #10)

15. my favorite sport are golf mr owen is a great coach

(From page 125, #17)

Cumulative Assessment (cont.)

16. at the cabin us goed fishing hikeing and swiming

(From page 139, #8)

17. how many tooths has you lost asked molly

(From page 139, #12)

18. knew leafs are comeing out on the trees said mrs wood

(From page 125, #1)

19.

2345 main st

dallas tx 76590

may 11 2005

dear grandpa

were leaving sunday four you're house sea you soon

with love

matt

(From page 139, #11)

Blank Sentence Form

Name: _____ Date: _____

_____

_____

_____

_____

_____

Name: _____ Date: _____

_____

_____

_____

_____

_____